As I Heal I Wrote
These Words

As I Heal I Wrote These Words

Phyllis L. Butler

AuthorHouse™ LLC
1663 Liberty Drive
Bloomington, IN 47403
www.authorhouse.com
Phone: 1-800-839-8640

Published by AuthorHouse   02/13/2014

ISBN: 978-1-4918-4683-4 (sc)
ISBN: 978-1-4918-4681-0 (hc)
ISBN: 978-1-4918-4682-7 (e)

Library of Congress Control Number: 2013923690

CONTENTS

ACKNOWLEDGEMENTS

First I would like to thank God for keeping me strong as I journeyed through life from a baby, a little girl and now a woman. You were there holding my hand in the mist of all my mistakes. You kept me safe from evil and you led the way. You cradled me in your arms when I felt no one else was there. And through it all you allowed me to meet some incredible people along the way. I cannot and I will not complain.

Sanjwelo Gallon III you are a remarkable man and best friend who taught me a lot about life. I can never forget our long chats on the phone. You remained true to the meaning of friendship many times over. I can never thank you enough.

Sabu C. Jose you are a very sweet friend who kept my spirits up when I was down. You pulled me through when I was at my lowest point. You helped soothe my pain by reading the Bible with me. You never got tired of me repeating my problems. You kept me focused on God.

Virgil Hughes II you are a true protector in every sense of the word. You allowed me to open up to you about my pain. You kept me focused on God. You continuously allowed me to shed tears and you were there to wipe them up by feeding me more and more scriptures. You are a true friend and Masonic brother. You were there for me then and now. You gave me so many words of encouragement. I will always remember you named me Loved One. You have a friend for life.

SGT Mark Kumi you selfishly fought for our country in Afghanistan. In addition, you took out the time to remind me of the wonderful blessings from God. You lifted my spirits and gave me hope. You never treated me like I was a woman that just "didn't get it." You spent many hours going over the Bible with me and praying. God only knows that is what it took to ease my pain.

Pastor TD Jakes I would like to thank you for your sermons, books and your DVDs and your contributions to the world. You have helped me ease my pain and gain understanding about God, life and relationships.

To the late TUPAC Amaru Shakur (1971-1996) because of you and your poem, "The Rose that Grew From Concrete" I started to understand my struggles in life and I started to view myself as a survivor. Your music kept me going and it pulled me through. I understood the messages you were sending especially your cry out to God. You definitely made a difference in my life. Tupac may you RIP with love Phyllis.

A BROKEN HEART

A broken heart is full of pain

Sometimes you will feel insane

Never give up and try to get better

Make it through the storm and rainy weather

Hold on to God's unchanging hand

Make sure you are wise in dealing with the next man

A broken heart can heal

Just make sure things are for real

Never letting go will cause you grief

Hold on to God and his beliefs

He will make your days brighter

He will make your load lighter

Give all your troubles to Him

You will see

You will win

A GAZE IN MY EYES

A Gaze in my eyes

Makes me realize

That you notice me

And that you really care

You will always be there for me

No worries

No doubts

Our love is something to shout about

WISHING I COULD TURN
BACK THE HANDS OF TIME

I wish I could turn back the hands of time

My heart would not ache and I would be fine

This pain is so unbearable

The way things happened

It was so terrible

When your heart did not meet

The same measure

I didn't have your love to treasure

Instead I hung in there

Trying to make it work

All my effort sweat and tears

Now things are very clear

You were not the one meant for me

Now I see

Now I see . . .

A HEART OF GOLD

A heart of gold

Can sometimes melt

Like hot candle wax

When people are harsh

And cut like an ax

Poor tender heart loving in all

Always trying to do right

But always fall

Remember the good

Remember the bad

They will remember the love

They once had

I'VE CARRIED
THIS LOAD FOR SO LONG

I've carried this load for so long

Can't figure out what I did wrong

Did you see any good in the things I've done?

Or did you feel better to run?

Never getting caught in my web of love

Never listening to God from above

Things were twisted there for a while

I felt lost and confused

Never never thought I would be used

Let me stand back up on both two feet

Be better than ever

Never a Defeat!!

FOR CHILDREN

You might not know this

You are too young

Everyone has feelings

So hold your tongue

The mean things you say

Can hurt them for life

They will try to heal

They will try to let go

Who knows how this will affect them?

You may never know

FOR PARENTS

Love your kids

They are a reflection of you

Teach them to have morals

Teach them to be kind

Let them know

They can shine

The time you invest in them will bring

Great honor to this world

HOW DID I FALL IN LOVE

I never felt this pain before

Was it love that is no more?

I can't understand this feeling inside

Too much of me is lost

Too much of me has died

If I could change the way I feel

My heart would be protected

My heart would be sealed

You may never know how I feel

Believe me it was true

Believe me it was real

Hopefully I will continue to grow

Hopefully I will heal

I don't know . . . .

I DIDN'T LOOK BEFORE I LEAPED

I didn't look before I leaped

Now I am sad and I weep

You were supposed to be there

But you didn't care

What can I do now?

It's time to pick up the pieces

Why didn't I see?

Your heart was not for me

I didn't look before I leaped

Now I am sad and I weep

When the days turn into nights

And I'm feeling all alone

All I can do is wonder

Where did I go wrong?

You are no longer here

My life is in despair

I didn't look before I leaped

Now I am sad and now I weep

I HAD TO PULL THROUGH IT

I had to pull through it

    When my heart was troubled

    And the pain was so deep

The road seemed SO long

    The mountains too steep

    I cried out to God to hold my hand

    A calling only for Him not man

    God came and healed my soul

I had to pull through it

When I thought nobody cared

God was right there to heal me again

I HAVE TO LET YOU GO

I have to let you go

Out of my heart and out of my soul

Live your life

With your brand new wife

I cannot complain about God's decision

He decided that we would not be as one

This road is hard and I will travel it alone

No looking back

No looking back

Keep moving with God holding my hand

I will have faith and I will STAND . . . .

KNOW YOUR WORTH

As the days pass by and you ask yourself why

Things are happening and what are the reasons

Remember in life there will be trouble in ALL seasons

SPRING to help you learn

SUMMER to help you grow

WINTER to move you in directions you never know

FALL to bring you back full circle so you can see how you have grown

How proud you will be at your strong inner self

Look at what God made

Remember your worth

23

LETTING GO

One of the hardest things for me

Was to sever something that

Was not meant to be

The pain was so unbearable and real

All my dreams shattered not at will

Where did I go wrong?

Was my love not good enough?

Your silence makes the pain go deeper

Makes me wonder if I am a Keeper

I ask God daily to show me the way

I am obedient just lost in life while looking

For an answer to my existence

LISTEN TO THE MUSIC

Music will soothe your soul

It will warm your body when you feel cold

Listen to the lyrics and hear the beat

Think of how the rhythm is sweet

Relaxation is what you will feel

A beat so enchanting and so real

Keep listening and enjoy the words

Music will soothe your soul

LOVED ONE

The Loved One is always there

She is grand and she is rare

Treat her well every day

Do those things to make her stay

Respect her well

All of the time

Never forget she is one of a kind

MY GOD MY GOD

My God My God

He watches over me

He protects me from all harm

I am blessed and I am free

Whenever I am down

Whenever I am hurt

My God lifts me up

He does his work

He wipes away all my tears

HIS love is so real

I have energy to go on

With My God's love

All the day long

MY HEART
SO WONDERFULLY MADE

My heart so wonderfully made

Is broken and in pain

Memories of you are still there

I wonder did you ever care

You never uttered a word of how you felt

I feel so lost, broken and hurt

Hopefully one day the pain will go away

Just let me have memories

No one can take them away

I wanted you to save me from my pain

But instead you walked away

I realize now you were hurting too

So you had no energy for me and you

God wants me to come to Him with praise

At the right time be loyal be strong

Be brave

MY ROAD WAS NOT EASY

My road was not easy

I didn't plan it that way

I didn't have a choice

In the matter

I didn't have any say

Yes I made decisions

I got over the bumps

I got over the curves

And all the twists and

Turns all in the road

What is at the end?

Will I win?

Yes I win!!!

NEVER FEEL ALONE

Never feel alone

Even when times may get rough

And you have a heavy load

All you see is hardship

And struggle on your road

Remember God will take your hand

Remember God for He has a plan

He will pull you through

Hold on tight and don't let go

Things will get better Go Go Go

All the hurt and pain that you just went through

Made you stronger and you will no longer

Feel sad and blue

STARTING TODAY

Starting today

I look at life in a different way

No more tears

No more pain

Any hurt I will refrain

Live happy, joyous and free

Keep smiling, keep shining

It's the only way to be

God has a hand in my life

Keep the faith to bring blessings to thee

SUCCEEDING IN LIFE

Succeeding in life

Takes a lot of will power

Enjoy it to the fullest

Enjoy every hour

Believe in yourself and never give up

Stand tall stand firm stand tough

Be positive in all that you do

You are so special and loving too

Succeeding in life

Takes a lot of will power

Enjoy yourself

Enjoy every hour

Make a difference starting today

Be ambitious show others the way

TAKE LIFE SERIOUSLY

As each day passes by

Listen, learn, create and try

Try to discover your inner self

Never, never worry about wealth

God's blessings will come to you

Keep your faith

Be very true

Remember people this isn't new

Take life seriously

Or life will seriously take you

THE PAST

The past has gone at last

No more crying

No more pain

I need to move on

Create another chapter in my life

A new beginning

A new view

It will be so different without you

THE PAIN OF THE PAST

Don't let the pain of the past last

Don't keep it alive in your heart

You must keep moving and never look back

Grow and become stronger don't ever slack

Your thoughts are your ways

Your ways are your ideas

Make a change

Turn it into reality

You will see how much

You shine

THERE IS NOTHING LEFT TO SAY

There is nothing left to say

You had your wedding day

All my dreams were shattered and torn

I felt so lonely and scorned

I kept it real as can be

I thought it was going to be you and me

You are gone now so much sorrow

For me I feel there is no tomorrow

I will fight to bring the joy again

One day I will be happy

One day I will win

49

TO THE MAN
THAT WAS MISUNDERSTOOD

Dedicated to the Late Tupac Amaru Shakur

To the man that was misunderstood

You grew up hard

You were raised in the hood

You spoke whatever was on your mind

You didn't hide

You didn't whine

Your lyrics were so meaningful

I thought you were so beautiful

I could feel your mood

I definitely understood

You were only trying to get your point across

You felt there was a lost

In the inner city for the youth

But you made it

You were the proof

That dreams can be reality

You still can have your dignity

Sad your life ended too soon

By a coward who misunderstood

You don't need a gun to win

A gun represents violence it reaps sin

51

WHEN I LOOK
AT THE MOUNTAINS

When I look at the mountains that God created

I see strength, dignity and confirmation that

God loves us eternally

He wants the best for you and me

No matter if the sun is out

No matter if it rains

Those mountains He created will remain

As a symbol of His love and dedication

Look at those mountains so strong and tall

Just like God's love for us all

WHEN IT RAINS OUTSIDE

When it rains outside

All I can do is cry

You are away

I sit and pray

I ask God to heal my heart

Comfort me in the dark

I hold on tight while on this painful ride

Wishing the pain would go away

Let me start all over again

WHY DID YOU HAVE TO BE SO COLD

It was just yesterday that you made me laugh

Now today I am sad with tears

I understand you didn't want to love me

But why did you have to be so cold?

When we were together we had so much fun

I was so happy I thought I was the only one

I thought I had your heart for a lifetime

I see I was wrong

I understand you didn't want to love me

But why did you have to be so cold?

A GROWING ROSE

A Growing Rose will always grow

Day after day night after night

Although it will encounter

The thunder and the rain

Its pain will never be in vain

The same measure of its endurance

Will be the same measure of its glorification

It will develop thorns

But it will never lose its beauty

It will encounter adversity

But it will never lose its smell

It will become stronger as time passes by

A growing rose is so beautiful and strong

No one will ever notice the things that went wrong

They will only notice the perky petals

And the strong stems

Never ever realizing there is pain within

A KEEPER

A keeper is someone that satisfies

Make sure you are happy

And realizes that

Happiness will make

You feel good inside

A keeper will be there for you

When you are sad and blue

Open their heart and stay true to you

A keeper is someone that

Treats you like a winner

Makes sure you aren't hungry

And fixes your dinner

A keeper fulfills your every need

Supports you totally without greed

If you meet someone that sounds like this

Don't let them go

You can hit or miss

A LASTING FRIENDHIP

A lasting friendship is the best kind

A type of friendship that takes time

Laughing, joking and sharing secrets

That's the lasting friendship you cannot measure

It's the kind of friendship you will always treasure

A bond so tight

A bond so rare

A lasting friendship shows you care

Your friendship is etched in gold

Your friendship will never get old

Hold your friendship dear to your heart

A lasting friendship will never part

A PEACEFUL MOMENT

A peaceful moment can be

Visions of a blue bird that sings

A cool breeze across your face

Twenty year old fine wine to taste

A peaceful moment can be receiving

A big hug with lots of love

A peaceful moment can be so many things

Enjoy them

A SET BACK IS MADE
FOR A COME BACK

Just the other day

A problem came my way

I felt there was something

I needed to do

Instead of pouting

And feeling blue

I decided to change the mood

I focused on a solution

Things got better

And I will never

Let a problem

Cause me to lack

That is why i know

A set back is made

For a come back

A SILENT MIND

A silent mind can still speak

A silent mind is never weak

Don't under estimate a person's ability

Just because they don't have your same agility

Get to know them before you judge

It's not good to have a grudge

They could be a wonderful person in your life

Just see how loving and kind they really are

A light shining bright

A shining star

Sometimes it takes your support

To reach the meek

A silent mind

May not speak

They are still human

And never weak

BE A WINNER NOT A SINNER

How easy it would be to set your mind free

Than constantly lie and talk down to thee

Control your unruly ways

Your lies

Your cheating and

Your theft

Make a change

Before you take your last breath

Ask God to show mercy on your soul

Change your ways

Be brave

Be bold

Do right by others

Before things get rough

Be a winner not a sinner

71

CREATE MY SMILE

Create my smile

When I see your face

Great moments of you in this place

We are holding hands

Listening to one another

You are my friend

You are my lover

Create my smile

It's only one of a kind

In that special place

In my mind

DIFFERENT THINGS

Different things motivate different people

Some like material things

Some like the steeple

Differences enhance our

Quality of living

Especially when

You are constantly giving

Accepting differences

Trying to understand

We may be different

But better than no man

Some like dancing

Some like romancing

Some like money

Some act funny

The world is full of people

That like different things

We are better off

Accepting those differences

By all means

DO YOU KNOW
WHO YOU REALLY ARE

Do you know who you really are?

When there are so many

Influences under the stars

Singers, actors, doctors and teachers

Don't forget the good old preacher

Being unique is a good reason

To view life's changes that is displeasing

Be your own person and love your ways

Your uniqueness will be admired someday

Live life happy

Rejoice all the time

Do you know who you really are?

God made you

Specially designed

EVERYONE HAS SOMETHING TO OFFER

Everyone has something to offer each other

Even though we may have a different mother

You can always learn something from people you meet

Learning something new is always a treat

Don't knock a subject you know nothing about

Look, listen and pay attention

Be ready to learn because you may have questions

Everyone has something to offer you'll see

Maybe you just missed the lesson that came from me

FAMILY LOVE

Family love has a strong bloodline

It runs deeper time after time

Mom is there right on top

Keeping the line strong there with pop

Brothers are there when needed no doubt

Sisters bring love to make you shout

Culturally and traditionally family love

Brings us closer together

You can see the strength

The smiles

The bond

The fun

Family love is number one

FORGIVING
SETS THE HEART FREE

Forgiving sets the heart free

No pain for you and no pain for me

Learning to see that we all make mistakes

Give your love instead of giving hate

A random act of kindness

Give it your all

That is easy than starting a brawl

Give a smile, a hug, a gift

Make people laugh

Give them a lift

You never know

What others are going through

Forgiving will make a difference

A difference for me and you

FUNNY HOW THINGS APPEAR

Funny how things appear

When we don't see what's in view very clear

You see something that is negative

When actually it's innocent

Take the time to access the situation

Get all facts and be patient

In time you will have all your answers

No more wondering

No more guessing

Before you know it

You will have no fear

What you are looking at

Will become very clear

HEY LITTLE BIRDIE

Hey little birdie tell me why

You fly gracefully

Through the sky

You are always on your way

You are a survivor every day

Gathering food or resting in your nest

You make it seem easy

You are the best

I know God has a handle on you

He makes sure you have food

Just like you He will take care of us

With our faith there is trust

No doubt God loves us

I AM A GIFT GIVER

I am a Gift Giver

I go the full mile

Enjoy your presents

I love to see you smile

It's not all about the material things

When you get a gift from me

There are no strings

I am a Gift Giver

I can deliver

God has blessed

Me totally

I am so humble

I am so free

Enjoy my token of appreciating you

Remember I am a Gift Giver

Full of life and so true

I GOT A CALLING

I got a calling

A calling from thee

To tell the whole world

How He died for me

This is why I am happy and free

I got a calling

A calling from thee

To tell the whole world

How He saved me

No more fears

Just glory to see

That is why I honor thee

I MAY NEVER HEAR YOU SAY YOU'RE SORRY

I may never hear you say you're sorry

For the things you've done

It was brutal

A battle

You on the run

You will never know what I went through

Crying my eyes out trying to get over you

God sent some angels to look after me

They were supportive and consoled thee

I owe it to God for pulling me through

I can honestly say He will never forget you

When you are in trouble

And can no longer bare

God is there

For He cares

IF I HAD MY WAY

If I had my way you would stay

We would live a good life and always pray

Asking God for grace from above

Asking Him to shower us with love

If I had my way you would stay

Be close by my side every day

We would both be happy

To face each day

If I had my way

IN THIS GAME CALLED LIFE

In this game called life

You enter a race

You win or lose

You run at your pace

Everyone will try to reach the finish line

Some will finish but at different times

Then there are some that will not finish at all

They gave up they didn't try at all

They didn't believe it to achieve it

They didn't take it to make it

In this game called life

KEEP ON MOVIN
UNTIL YOU ARE FREE

When your heart is heavy

Keep on movin until you are free

Free of the pain and you can see

See clearer and know that what

You are feeling is normal

Pain in your heart

Can come at any time

Especially when

You can't find

Someone to take your love seriously

Keep on movin until you are free

As time goes on

It will easily

Get better

LEARN FROM OTHERS

Learn from others and get some advice

This is one way not to do things twice

See their actions good or bad

This is a classroom for any lad

You can learn from anyone

Your mother, father, sister, brother or friend

See the things they do and you will win

Win a chance to learn something for free

Something that is valuable you will see

LET ME SEE
THE GOOD SIDE OF YOU

Let's talk like we just met for the very first time

Let's feel relaxed and let's feel fine

I know there are a lot of things we can do

We both can have fun just me and you

Let me see the good side of you

The side that brings joy

The side that is true

I know you care enough

Like a lover would

Let me see the good side of you

LOVE IS A FEELING

Love is a feeling from deep down inside

It makes you stand tall and full of pride

Knowing your mind has a desire

To cradle someone and to admire

You can smile daily and feel great

Having love to reciprocate

Two hearts that beat as one

Love is a feeling from deep inside

To let the world know

You are happy this time

Let the world know

You are fine

MY FUTURE GOALS

My future goals

Are so extraordinary

I dream in making things happen

Yet on the contrary

Setting the example

Will be my fate

To show others what it takes

To obtain all you set out to do

Believe in God

He'll bless you

Believe me

Take one step

He'll take three

NO MATTER WHAT
DON'T RELY ON LUCK

No matter what

Don't rely on luck

Base things on reality

Pray to God for stability

He knows what his plan is for you

He knows what you need to do

Put Him first

In all you do

This will be a blessing

For me and you

PUT GOD FIRST

Put God first whatever you do

Don't forget his kindness

And blessings too

He is there for you every day

Just like He helped Moses led the way

When you have reached a point in your life

When you are troubled and full of strife

God has a way of showing up

Only when he says that's enough

You will be taken care of

See how He works

All you have to do is put God first

SHOWING YOU I CARE

Showing you I care

Doesn't make me weak

It's the little things I do

Don't you think?

Giving you gifts from my heart

Eases the strain while we're apart

You were the one

Under the sun

Showing you I care

Making you aware

That I * Love * You

SOMETIMES I NEED A LIFT

There will be days when I feel down

No talking, no laughing don't want anyone around

That is the time I need some peace to myself

I sit; I pray and think of God's grace

Sometimes I need a lift

During this time

Come to me, support me and I'll be fine

Take me by the hand

Help me understand

That you are there

To lift me up

115

TEACH ME HOW TO LOVE YOU

There will be times in my life

I might not do the right thing

I will keep trying

I will try to bring

Joy in your life

I might not know

You feel a different way

A different way to go

Teach me how to love you

I will do my very best

I will stay busy

I will not take a rest

You come first

In my life

I want things for the better

Not for the worst

THE BEAUTY OF NATURE

The beauty of nature is so lovely to see

A calm free flowing maple tree

Beautiful flowers all pretty in bloom

Makes you cheerful forget your gloom

The sun is shining

It's great timing

For us to enjoy

The fresh air

The sounds of the birds singing a happy melody

Makes you feel welcome in harmony

The beauty of nature is so nice

You are amazed and put in a daze while viewing the

World's playground

THE CLOUDS IN THE SKY

The clouds in the sky

Take my breath away

They are so bright

I enjoy this day

I wish I could feel them

Right in my hands

The clouds in the sky

Made by God

Amen

THE ONLY WAY TO GO

The only way to go

Would be on the right road

Steer clear of a bad direction

Move carefully don't be scared

Stay focus on your ways to get ahead

Positive actions

Reap positive results

Negative actions

Reap too many faults

Life has a way of teaching us lessons

The best student makes the best impressions

As you see the fruit of your labor

People will say you received favor

From God the Protector of us all

He is the one pushing you along

Keeping you straight and

Keeping you strong

THE RAINBOW
SYMBOLIZES HIS LOVE

The rainbow symbolizes His love

God has His grace on us from above

He lets us know His presence is near

When we feel lonely He is there

There is no need to worry

There is no need to fear

Sometimes after the rain

You can look out your window pane

And see the colorful spectrum in view

Red, yellow, green, violet, orange and blue

A seal of the covenant between God and us

Never will flood waters destroy all of the earth

The rainbow is a message sent from above

The symbolization of His love

TIT BUT NO TAT

Tit but no tat

You hurt me

I do no tat

I prayed for you today

There was no reason to go the negative way

Tit but no tat

You lied on me

I do no tat

I prayed for you today

There was no reason to go the negative way

God will fight my battles every day

TOUGH TIMES
MAKE YOU STRONGER

Have you ever notice

When times are tough

You pull right through

And that's enough

To show you all the things

You did wrong

Now you start to do things

In different way

Thus not to repeat

The mistakes of yesterday

You'll work harder

You'll work smarter

And things are not so bad

Tough times make you stronger

WHAT REALLY IS A WINNER

Could it be that I just can't see

What really is a winner?

In life we take score

Only to ignore

The things we saw in the beginning

An effort is made

A skill is displayed

Eager to reach the top

The only problem with this

The one that was left behind is

Looked down upon as a flop

See when losing a game

There are many lessons to gain

You learn what not to do

The next time you are a contestant

WHEN OUR LIVES
GO THEIR SEPARATE WAYS

When our lives go their separate ways

There is a time of pain

You are no longer here

To fulfill my dreams

I definitely feel the strain

I want to scream

You are out of my life

I must fight this

It's not right

This little twist of fate

I see it is too late

I cannot control this

I fall to my knees

And even if I say please

I know it will not bring you back

133

WHEN YOU LOVE YOURSELF

When you love yourself

See how amazing

You will feel inside

So keep blazing

Acquire the things you desire

Enjoy life and be admired

Maintain your strength and your perseverance

Don't let anything or anyone cause interference

Set your goals one by one

Never stop until you're done

Live your life

To the fullest every day

Learn from your mistakes

That's the only way

When you love yourself

Things will fall in place

When you love yourself

You can LOVE the ENTIRE RACE

135

YOU WILL ALWAYS
BE A DIAMOND

You will always be a diamond

Even when not seen

Your positiveness will still remain

Even when others are mean

Never lose your focus

Never lose hope

One day your light will shine

Brighter than you thought

You will entertain others

Teach them to have fun

You will always be a diamond

You will be number one

YOUR SONG YOUR RHYTHM

Your song

Your rhythm

Your dance

Your feet

Makes me wonder whose beat

Keep striving for life's dreams

Maintain your self esteem

Lift others as much as you can

Remain strong and keep a stand

For In life we are all winners

Moving to our own pace

Still trying to finish the race

Of Life and Liberty

Your song

Your rhythm

Your dance

Your feet

ABOUT THE AUTHOR

PHYLLIS L. BUTLER is originally from Maryland and currently resides in Houston, Texas. She is the proud daughter of Carolyn L. Thompson and Joseph R. Butler Sr. She knew at an early age that she would some day write a novel. She really enjoys writing and already has plans for future projects. She hopes one day her novels will make it to the big screen in Hollywood. Writing is her new found hobby and she dreams of one day entertaining the entire world.